Electricity
from COAL

Making electricity

We can make electricity.

We can make electricity with the sun and the wind.

3

Electricity from coal

Look at the **coal**.

We can make electricity with the coal too.

5

Burning coal

Look at the coal.

We can burn the coal.

Hot water

Look at the fire.

The fire will burn.

The fire will burn
and make the water hot.

Steam

Can you see the **steam**?

The steam is hot.

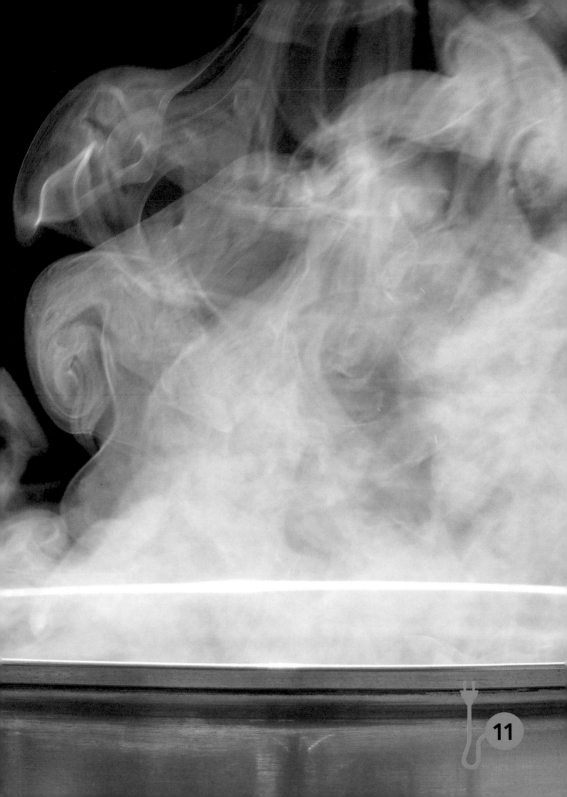

The steam will
go on the wheel.
The steam will make the
wheel go round and round.
This will make electricity.

The electricity is made here.

Glossary

coal

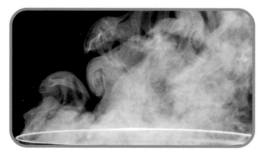

steam